PEOPLE BUILD
DAMS

Trent Johnson

PEOPLE BUILD DAMS.

4

SO DO BEAVERS.

PEOPLE BUILD TOWERS.

So do termites.

PEOPLE BUILD TUNNELS.

SO DO MOLES.

PEOPLE BUILD PLACES TO STORE FOOD.

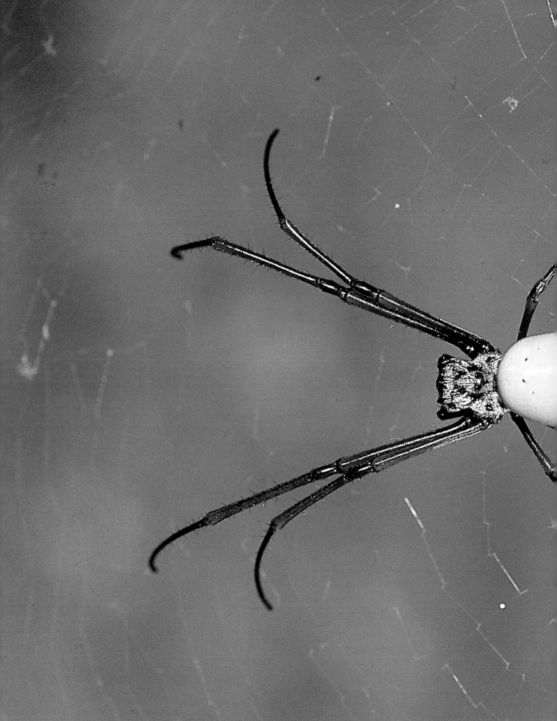

So do spiders.

PEOPLE BUILD HOUSES

WITH MANY ROOMS.

SO DO ANTS.

People build places to keep babies safe.

SO DO EAGLES.